Gilt-edged Splendour
Masterpieces in Silver Gilt

Koopman Rare Art 2013

Koopman Rare Art
53–64 Chancery Lane
London WC2A 1QS

Tel: 020 7242 7624
enquiries@koopmanrareart.com
www.koopmanrareart.com

Cat. no. 9

FOREWORD

When you enter a gallery or antique shop you are usually welcomed with the words: "How can I help you?" Walk into our shop and the question seems almost superfluous, for the selection of antique silver you find there is one of the best in the world and we have every confidence we can serve you.

Surrounding ourselves with lovely things can bring immense joy to our lives; the objects we collect are an antidote to the barrage of bad news constantly assailing us and, what is more, they have the potential to be a hedge against inflation. Great silver remains one of the favourite ways to enhance a collection. Touching and viewing these astonishing creative objects bring pleasure and remind us of skills long forgotten.

Sometimes people ask us: "What is the absolute best?" Silver-gilt items are very often high on the list. The collection that we offer in this catalogue shows that over many centuries patrons have gilded their finest silver to embellish and protect what they hold dear.

Our website will always give you a good idea of what silver and silver gilt we currently have in stock. But a visit to our gallery or to our stand at one of the antique fairs where we exhibit each year will give you an even better idea of the magnificent silver gilt we have for sale.

Lewis Smith
lewis@koopmanrareart.com

Cat. no. 8

INTRODUCTION

Return of the Golden Era

BY TIMO KOOPMAN

Man has long been fascinated with the glitter of gold, but its high cost and great softness rendered it impractical for many purposes. Demand for this precious metal drove silversmiths down the ages to devise methods of applying a gold finish to silver. Since ancient times gilding has enhanced silver objects, and items that have undergone that process are called silver gilt, or *vermeil* in French.

There are various methods of gilding, some more dangerous than others. That used in pre-Columbian South America by the Incas was depletion gilding, producing a layer of nearly pure gold on an object of gold alloy by the removal of the other metals from its surface. Another method is overlaying, or the folding of gold leaf, as mentioned in Homer's *Odyssey*. A third is fire gilding with mercury which involves applying an amalgam of gold and mercury to a silver surface. Heat volatizes the mercury and bonds a strong layer of gold to the silver. Although dangerous for the worker, this method, dating back to the sixth century BC, was used until comparatively recently. It has now been superseded almost entirely by electroplating in which electrolysis is used to coat the surface with gold.

The process of gilding, however, was costly. While in 1664 Samuel Pepys complained that the cost of "fashion", or the making of a piece, had risen to the same level as the raw material itself (both were 5 shillings an ounce), gilding the finished article could cost an additional 3 shillings an ounce. In 2007 we owned a fine pair of silver-gilt baskets made in London, 1766–7, by Parker and Wakelin. Documentation from the time shows that gilding added approximately 25 per cent to the total cost; this was considerably more than commissioning an object in silver yet still less than one in gold. By the Middle Ages, European gold was worth ten to twelve times more than silver, but by the eighteenth and nineteenth centuries the price ratio had risen to fifteen to one. Even so, achieving the golden look through gilding became ever more popular.

INTRODUCTION

Silver-gilt objects were often used as status symbols, as exemplified by a painting of the Guildhall Banquet held in 1814 for the Prince Regent, the Tsar of Russia and the King of Prussia. One dinner service is in silver gilt and the other quite intentionally in silver: guests seated with the silver-gilt service are "superior" to those with the silver service.

However, in French silver, many of the important services that have survived to date are entirely in silver gilt. Take for example the early nineteenth-century services for General Count François-Xavier Branicki, or for Count Nikolai Demidoff, or indeed the Borghese service or that made for Madame Mère, the mother of Napoleon. These grand dinner services were all produced by Jean-Baptiste-Claude Odiot and Martin-Guillaume Biennais, both of whom executed imperial commissions.

In this period popularity of silver-gilt items soared on both sides of the Channel, with the English royal goldsmiths Rundell, Bridge & Rundell and master silversmiths Paul Storr and Benjamin Smith leading the way. Their most important patrons were King George III, the Prince Regent (later George IV) and various children of the royal family.

Gold, unlike silver, is neither affected by the corrosiveness of salt nor by discoloration by sulphur, nor indeed by the acidity of many of the desserts that were popular at this time. Both silver and silver-gilt dessert services were thus used not merely to denote status but also for a practical reason: after the main course was served on plain silver, the main service was replaced or complemented by the silver-gilt dessert service, sometimes with diners adjourning to a separate room for dessert.

Aside from being less expensive than gold, silver-gilt items are lighter in weight and much more durable. Therefore many delicate objects were made in silver gilt. The nef (cf. the Burghley nef) is a dinner-table ornament or utilitarian vessel in the form of a ship. It dates from the thirteenth to the sixteenth century and was used as a drinking vessel or salt cellar. Indeed the salt cellar is where silver gilt truly excelled. From medieval times, people

Cat. no. 13

Cat. no. 15

recognized the importance of salt as a preservative. Elaborate and grand vessels were made to sit on the table before the master of the house. The expression "right hand man" used today derives from one's position at the table in relation to the salt cellar.

In Renaissance Europe the cabinets of curiosities (*Wunderkammern*) of noble households held vast collections in which many wonders from the New World, such as shells, mother of pearl and precious or semi-precious stones, were mounted in silver gilt to set off their beauty and flaunt the knowledge of their owners. Being silver gilt greatly reduced the need to clean and polish them, for gold tarnishes far more slowly than silver. This reduced the risk of an object being damaged, and often gilded items have survived in better condition than their silver counterparts.

We are delighted to present this magnificent collection of silver-gilt objects dating from the sixteenth to the twentieth century. Each masterpiece highlights not only the splendour and richness of gilded silver, but also reflects the socio-economic importance that it has always held.

Email: timo@koopmanrareart.com

The J. Pierpont Morgan **cup** and **cover**

Silver gilt
London, 1578
Maker's mark a bird in a shaped shield, probably for Afable Partridge
Height: 9¾ in (24.8 cm)

PROVENANCE
The Maskell Collection
J. Maskell, dec'd, Christie's, London, 25 July 1890
T.W. Waller, dec'd, Christie's, London, 7 June 1910, lot 68
J. Pierpont Morgan, by descent until 2010

EXHIBITED
London, 1862: *Special Exhibition of Works of Art of the Medieval, Renaissance, and More Recent Periods on Loan at the South Kensington Museum,* South Kensington Museum, London, exhibited from the Maskell Collection
London, 1901: *Exhibition of a Collection of Silversmiths' Work of European Origin*, Burlington Fine Arts Club, London, exhibited by T.W. Waller, Esq.

PUBLISHED
J. Starkie Gardner, ed., *Exhibition of a Collection of Silversmiths' Work of European Origin*, exh. cat., Burlington Fine Arts Club, London, 1901, no. 5, Case B, p. 10

This cup was part of the distinguished collection formed by William Maskell (1814–1890) in the middle years of the nineteenth century. Maskell was a noted medieval scholar and author, some of whose manuscripts are in the Bodleian Library, Oxford University. A number of items from his varied collections, including this spectacular cup, were on loan in the 1860s and 70s to the South Kensington Museum, which later became the Victoria and Albert Museum, and today the museum retains a dozen important works of art originally owned by him.

On Maskell's death in 1890, the cup was acquired by another distinguished collector, T.W. Waller of Westbourne Street, Paddington. He lent the cup to the highly influential exhibition of silver held in 1901 at Burlington House, and, after his death, the cup was acquired by J. Pierpont Morgan, the greatest of all American collectors. Morgan's collections formed the bases of several important museum collections in the United States including the Metropolitan Museum of Art in New York, the Wadsworth Atheneum in Hartford, Connecticut, and the Morgan Library. There were also landmark sales of items from his collections at Parke-Bernet in 1947 and Christie's in 1982. This cup, however, was retained by his descendants and remained in the family until 2010, when it was acquired privately by us.

Purchased by Leeds Museums and Galleries (Temple Newsam House) from the Mrs Patricia Hurst Bequest Fund in memory of herself and her husband

Four ice pails

Silver gilt
London, 1769
Maker's mark of **the Royal Goldsmith Thomas Heming**
Height: 7⅛ in (17 cm)
Weight: 187 oz (5,860 g)

HERALDRY
The arms are those of Carroll or O'Carroll of Ireland, descended from Sir Maolroona O'Carroll, Chief of His Name, knighted in 1603. Charles Carroll of Carrollton was a wealthy Maryland planter and last surviving signatory of the Declaration of Independence.

These elegant ice pails are amongst the earliest of this new form of wine cooler introduced from France in the middle years of the eighteenth century. Sets of four ice pails from this period are exceedingly rare.

3

Footed salver

Silver gilt
London, 1701
Maker's mark of **Anthony Nelme**
Diameter: 13½ in (34.2 cm)
Weight: 52 oz (1,631 g)

HERALDRY
The arms are those of Grenville accolé with Leofric quartering Temple, for Richard Grenville (1678–1727) and his wife Hester (d. 1752), sister of Sir Richard Temple, 5th Baronet of Stowe, later created 1st Viscount Cobham. They were married in 1710. On the death of Viscount Cobham Hester succeeded her brother to the Stowe estates and was created Countess Temple.

PROVENANCE
Richard Grenville (1678–1727) of Wotton Underwood, Buckinghamshire and by descent to
Richard Plantagenet, 2nd Duke of Buckingham (1797–1861), Stowe House, house sale, Christie's, 15 August 1848 and for the following 37 days, the 16th day, lot 146
Edward, 22nd Baron Hastings (b. 1912), Christie's, London, 9 December 1959, lot 155
Lord Harris of Peckham

A salver was defined in a 1661 dictionary as "a new peece of wrought plate, broad and flat, with a foot underneath, and is used in giving Beer or other liquid to save the Carpitt or Cloathes from drops".

4

Pair of two-handled **bowls** and **covers**

Silver gilt
London, c. 1710
Maker's mark of **Pierre Platel**
The undersides of the bowls with scratch weights *19-15* and *19-17*
Length (over handles): 6½ in (16.5 cm)
Weight: 39 oz 7 dwt (1,125 g)

PROVENANCE
Thomas Hugh Cobb, Sotheby's, London, 19 October 1944, lot 70
The Property of a Gentleman, Christie's, London, 9 October 1957, lot 154
The Estate of Donald S. Morrison, Sotheby Parke-Bernet, New York, 6 June 1980, lot 49

EXHIBITED
Princeton, New Jersey, 1966: *English Silver*, Princeton University Art Museum, Princeton, New Jersey, cat. no. 16
Brooklyn, New York, 1958–1980: The Brooklyn Museum, loan no. L58.4.5.6

PUBLISHED
The Magazine Antiques, May, 1964
The Magazine Antiques, December, 1971

Made in Platel's workshop during the period when Paul de Lamerie was serving his apprenticeship there, these bowls may well be very early works by de Lamerie.

T.H. Cobb was sometime partner in Janson, Cobb, Pearson & Co., solicitors of 22 College Hill, London, from which firm he retired on 1 December 1929. Among the bequests he made in 1944 to the Victoria and Albert Museum were the portrait of an unknown man, aged 22, by Nicholas Hilliard, 1597, and a silver chocolate pot, marked by John Fawdery, London, 1714.

5

Tea urn
After a design by **Jean-Jacques Boileau**

Silver gilt
London, 1806
Maker's mark of **Digby Scott & Benjamin Smith**, retailed by Rundell, Bridge & Rundell
The base stamped RUNDELL BRIDGE ET RUNDELL AURIFICES REGIS ET PRINCIPIS WALLIÆ LONDINI FECERUNT
Height: 14½ in (36.9 cm)
Gross weight: 241 oz 12 dwt (7,513 g)

PROVENANCE
C. Ruxton Love, New York City
The Audrey B. Love Foundation, Christie's, New York, 14 June 1982, lot 132
His Excellency Mahdi Mohammed Al-Tajir

EXHIBITED
London, 1989: *The Glory of the Goldsmith, Magnificent Gold and Silver from the Al-Tajir Collection*, Christie's, London, no. 121

PUBLISHED
J.B. Hawkins, *The Al-Tajir Collection of Silver and Gold*, London, 1983, pp. 108–9
M. Clayton, *Christie's Pictorial History of English and American Silver*, Oxford, 1985, p. 211, no. 3
The Glory of the Goldsmith, Magnificent Gold and Silver from the Al-Tajir Collection, exh. cat., London, 1989, pp. 158–9
A. Phillips and J. Sloane, *Antiquity Revisited, English and French Silver-Gilt from the Collection of Audrey Love*, London, 1997, pp. 7–8

This tea urn is typical of the Egyptomania that took England by storm in the early years of the nineteenth century. *Voyage dans la Basse et la Haute Egypte pendant les campagnes du Général Bonaparte*, the book of views of Egyptian antiquities published in Paris in 1802 by Baron Vivant Denon, Napoleon's cultural arbiter, was one of several books which provided models for Egyptian decoration in English silver. Rundell's designers happily blended these with Greek and Roman motifs to come up with a style that was both exotic and monumental, and provided models for the tea-table as well as the dining-room. Similar winged paw feet are found on salts, sauce-boats, and candelabra.

The draughtsman responsible for providing these designs to Rundell's was probably Jean-Jacques Boileau, a French artist who came to London in the 1790s to work at Carlton House, the sumptuous palace the Prince of Wales was decorating in London. His success lay in creating a style that was at once imposing and elegant. The crisp stiff foliage of the borders on the tea urn provides a pleasing contrast to the burnished plain surfaces of the body.

The Regency period was dominated by the retail firm of Rundell, Bridge & Rundell, Goldsmiths to the King and the Prince of Wales. Although Philip Rundell trained as a jeweller, he was also astute in business and quick to take advantage of the growing prosperity in the early years of the nineteenth century. In addition, the nation's military and naval successes led to many celebratory commissions. Rundell's partner John Bridge employed the best artists and designers of the day, including the sculptors John Flaxman and Edward Hodges Baily, and it was their designs, many of which were for monumental pieces in the Roman and Egyptian styles, which led to Rundell's position as the pre-eminent supplier of silver gilt to the royal family, the aristocracy and gentry.

6

Tray

Silver gilt
London, 1791
Maker's mark of **James Young**
Length: 29 in (74.5 cm)
Weight: 296 oz (9,206 g)

HERALDRY
The arms are those of Hamilton, for John James Hamilton,
9th Earl of Abercorn, created Marquess of Abercorn in 1790.

PROVENANCE
John James Hamilton, 1st Marquess of Abercorn (1756–1818)
The Property of a Gentleman, Sotheby's, London,
25 October 1962, lot 126
Sotheby's, London, 9 April 1964, lot 127
Hilmar Reksten, Christie's, London, 22 May 1991, lot 38

PUBLISHED
Stanley C. Dixon, *English Decorated Trays*, 1964, illustrated p. 13
Hilmar Rekstens Samlinger, Bergen, 1978, p. 146
Christie's Review of the Season, 1991, illustrated p. 186

James Young was responsible for some of the most impressive silver produced during the last decades of the eighteenth century, including two magnificent centrepieces with a marine theme. One of these, made in 1786 for John Fitzgibbon, later Earl of Clare, was sold by us a few years ago. Another exceptional example of Young's work is this tray. Fine by any standards of salver and tray making, it is also expertly and boldly engraved within a border of excellently rendered rosettes and scrolled foliage in bright-cut.

Although the engraver responsible for the decoration on this tray is not known, the eminent scholar John Culme has suggested that it may have been engraved in the studio of John Thompson (d. 1801) of 44 Gutter Lane, which was a few minutes' walk from Young's workshops at 70 Little Britain.

7

Royal ewer and basin

Silver gilt
London, 1820
Maker's mark of **William Elliott**
Basin width: 15¼ in (38.7 cm)
Ewer height: 10 in (25.4 cm)
Weight: 69 oz 10 dwt (2,176 g)

HERALDRY
The Royal Arms are those borne by Princess Sophia, the fifth of the six daughters of George III and Queen Charlotte.

PROVENANCE
H.R.H. Princess Sophia (1777–1848), daughter of George III
Probably sold on her death to Garrard's
Lord Harris of Peckham

Queen Charlotte was protective of her daughters, attempting to shield them from marriage, and limit their suitors. Princess Sophia never married, though she did form an attachment to Major-General Thomas Garth (1744–1828). In 1800, she bore him a son named Thomas (d. 1875), whom Garth raised at Weymouth.

After her mother's death in 1818, Princess Sophia lived at Kensington Palace in Vicarage Place and became a close confidante of the Duchess of Kent, Queen Victoria's mother. Princess Sophia and the Duchess formed an alliance with Sir John Conroy, who eventually embezzled most of the Princess's money.

Following her death in 1848, Princess Sophia's jewellery and silver were together valued by Garrard's at £6,728 2s 6d, and much of it was divided between her four surviving siblings. The remaining plate was sold by Garrard's in 1848 for £1,012 17s 6d.

22 | Koopman Rare Art

8

Two-handled tray

Silver gilt
London, 1804
Maker's mark of **Benjamin Smith**, retailed by Rundell, Bridge & Rundell
Width across handles: 31 in (79 cm)
Weight: 256 oz (7,962 g)

HERALDRY
The armorials are those of Thomas, 3rd Baron Foley (1780–1833).

PROVENANCE
Thomas, 3rd Baron Foley (1780–1833)
By descent to Gerald Henry, 7th Baron Foley (1898–1927), house sale, Ruxley Lodge, Claygate, Surrey, Castiglione & Scott, 14 October 1919 and six following days, lot 1329
Private Collection, New York

Thomas Foley, 3rd Baron Foley (1780–1833) was the son of the 2nd Baron Foley and his wife Henrietta Stanhope. He succeeded his father in 1793, though was only able to take his seat in the House of Lords on gaining his majority in 1801. His father had been a notorious gambler of whom it was said that "by a most rapid course of debauchery, extravagance and gaming [he] rendered one of the most noblest fortunes in the kingdom abortive". The 3rd Baron's marriage at the age of twenty-six to Lady Cecilia FitzGerald, daughter of the Duke of Leinster, no doubt improved the family fortunes, and this tray, originally one of a pair and part of a large suite of silver gilt, was likely part of their wedding plate.

9

Four candlesticks

Silver gilt
Paris, 1809–1819
Maker's mark of **Jean-Baptiste-Claude Odiot**
Height: 8 in (22 cm)
Weight: 59 oz (1,862 g)

PROVENANCE
A Washington Collector, Christie's, New York,
5 October 1983, lot 45
His Excellency Mahdi Mohammed Al-Tajir

PUBLISHED
Catherine Barnett, "Old Flames: A Panorama of English, French, and American Silver Candlesticks", *Art & Antiques Magazine*, January, 1985, p. 66

The elegant caryatid supports for these candlesticks owe their inspiration to Renaissance models, which in turn were inspired by the female columns of the Erechtheum of the Acropolis. In the third quarter of the sixteenth century Pierre Lescot and Jean Goujon designed four caryatids supporting an entablature in the Salle des Caryatides in the Louvre.

10

Pair of **soup tureens, covers** and **stands**

Silver gilt
Paris, 1798–1809
Maker's mark of **Martin-Guillaume Biennais**
Engraved on underside *No 1-24^{M}2^{O}7^G* and
No 2-24^M-5°-4^G
Width: 17½ in (44.4 cm)
Weight: 384 oz 12 dwt (11,960 g)

HERALDRY
The arms are those of Saavedra for Francisco Saavedra de Sangronis (1749–1819).

The tureens have all the qualities of the greatest French silver of the period which the late Shirley Bury, curator at the Victoria and Albert Museum, described as exhibiting "strong profiles scarcely interrupted by disciplined ornament, sometimes polished on a matted ground, and frequently enhanced by cast sculptural elements". The beauty of these tureens relies on the purity of their line and the considered but comparatively sparse applied decoration contrasting with the beauty of the plain burnished surfaces. The chasing on the covers has a subtle sophistication.

The tureens are after a design by Charles Percier and Pierre-François-Léonard Fontaine, whose published work, thanks to their position as architects to Napoleon, had huge influence on silver designs of the period. Anthony Phillips and Jeanne Sloane have observed that "the work of Percier and Fontaine was perhaps best interpreted in the world of silver by the firm of Martin-Guillaume Biennais".

The name of Martin-Guillaume Biennais (1764–1843) is synonymous with the Empire period in France. His career, which began during the last years of the monarchy, was initially that of a *marchand-ébéniste* supplying *nécessaires de voyage* or boxed travelling services. He won the patronage of Napoleon and his family and went on to

supply him and the imperial household with large quantities of silver of the highest quality as well as furniture. Biennais employed over six hundred workmen, who were responsible for producing table services, swords, the Imperial coronation regalia, cabinets and shoe buckles. Some years ago, Clare Le Corbeiller of the Metropolitan Museum of Art in New York, which has a number of fine works by Biennais, commented: "In view of his background, the consistent refinement and elegance of his work in silver is remarkable". Biennais had premises at the sign of "Le Singe violet" [the Purple Monkey] in the rue Saint-Honoré; he employed the monkey on his hallmark. He supplied vast and imposing services to Grand Duke Mikhail Pavlovich and Tsar Alexander I as well as making the famous Borghese Service. We have sold important pieces from all these services during the past few years but this is the first time we have offered these tureens for sale.

Francisco Saavedra was born in Seville and trained as a doctor, although he changed career and went to work in the Ministry of the Indies. In 1780, while sailing to Havana, he was captured by the British and sent to Jamaica but released a year later. Once in Havana, Saavedra went on to meet the French admiral de Grasse in the French colony of St Domingue to agree on how best to help the French and American forces in the Revolutionary War. It was decided that their best course of action would be to attack the British forces in Virginia under Lord Cornwallis and then to attempt to regain control of British colonies in the Caribbean and most importantly Jamaica. Following the defeat of the French at the Battle of the Saintes in 1782 and the rising costs of the project, the Spanish decided to abandon this scheme and Saavedra was appointed governor of Caracas. He returned to Spain and served on the Supreme War Council and in 1797 was appointed Finance Minister and then in 1798 Minister of State. When his health failed he retired to Andalucía. It would not have been surprising that a diplomat with such close links to France at this time should have chosen to purchase his plate from a leading silversmith such as Biennais. Nevertheless it is possible that the tureens were a gift from the French hoping to retain Saavedra's sympathies and to encourage him to press the Spaniards into helping them against the British.

11

Twelve **shell dishes**

Silver gilt
Paris, 1798–1809
Maker's mark of **Jean-Baptiste-Claude Odiot**, also struck with a later Austrian tax mark
Width: 3½ in (9 cm)
Weight: 30 oz 7 dwt (945 g)

Shell dishes first appear in France at the end of the seventeenth century. In 1727 the Francophile Earl of Chesterfield received "sevon scallop shells" as part of the dinner service he took with him as ambassador to The Hague. Oyster sauce was a popular accompaniment to roast meats and it is possible that shells like these were filled with sauce and set around the table. They may also have been used for eating oysters as a *gratin*. A 1723 recipe directs: "Lay a piece of Sweet Butter at the Bottom of your Silver Scallop Shell; then get a quantity of Large Oysters, and cut off the fins; put four in a shell, with some of their own liquor strain'd, grated Bread, a little Salt, Pepper, and a spoonful of white wine, and cover them with grated Bread, and set them over your stove to stew; and hold over them your Browning-Iron; half an hour will stew them." Empire period examples are extremely rare.

12

Pair of unique dessert stands

Silver gilt, glass
London, 1821
Maker's mark of **Philip Rundell**,
retailed by Rundell, Bridge & Rundell
Stamped *RUNDELL BRIDGE ET RUNDELL AURIFICES REGIS LONDINI*
Width: 8¾ in (22 cm) square
Weight (excluding glass): 93 oz 3 dwt (2,898 g)

HERALDRY
The arms are those of Sutton for Sir Richard Sutton, 2nd Bt. (1799–1855).

PROVENANCE
Sir Richard Sutton 2nd Bt. (1798–1855), then by descent to Sir Richard Vincent Sutton 5th Bt. (1853–1918)
The Trustees of the Late Sir R.V. Sutton, Bt., Christie's, London, 31 March 1976, lot 124 (part)

The Sutton Service, purchased from the Royal Goldsmiths by Sir Richard Sutton in the years following his twenty-first birthday, was one of the largest and most impressive of the great silver-gilt services. Many of the pieces, such as these glass-lined dessert stands, are unusual in form and decoration, and all are of superb quality. Sutton inherited considerable estates in the Midlands and in Norfolk as well as London real estate at the age of four in 1802. He devoted his life to sport. In fox hunting it was said that "he never had an equal".

13

Epergne

Silver gilt
London, 1823
Maker's mark of **Benjamin Smith III**
Width: 23¼ in (59.1 cm)
Weight (excluding glass): 168 oz 4 dwt (5,231g)

During the early years of the nineteenth century, dinner still tended to be of three prodigious courses. The first two were served on white silver placed on a white tablecloth, but for the final, or dessert, course, the cloth was removed and a splendid array of silver gilt graced the glowing mahogany of the table top.

This magnificent centrepiece has three double candle branches which can be replaced by cut-glass dishes for luncheon.

14

Four wine coolers
After the Medici Vase

Silver gilt
London, 1811–12
Maker's mark of **Paul Storr**,
retailed by Rundell, Bridge & Rundell
Stamped *RUNDELL, BRIDGE ET RUNDELL AURIFICES REGIS ET PRINCIPES WALLIÆ LONDINI*
Height: 11¼ in (28.5 cm)
Weight: 684 oz (21,585 g)

PROVENANCE
Richard Howe, 1st Earl Howe (1796–1870)
By descent to Francis, 5th Earl Howe, Christie's, London, 1 July 1953
Charles and Fay Plohn, New York City
Mrs Fay Plohn, Sotheby's, London, 15 October 1970, lot 8
Private Collection
His Excellency Mahdi Mohammed Al-Tajir

Whereas the general form of these superb wine coolers is based on the Medici vase as engraved by G.B. Piranesi, the applied relief of the Triumph of Bacchus is derived from a Roman sarcophagus in the Vatican Museum. The sarcophagus was engraved by E.Q. Visconti and published in 1788. While we know that the Storr workshop held a number of Piranesi engravings, it seems almost certain that the workshop (or the firm's retailers Rundell's) also owned copies of Montfaucon's *Antiquity Explained*, published in England in 1721, as well as Visconti's engraving. All these publications were used as source material by designers for Rundell's and their working silversmiths such as William Pitts and Paul Storr.

The version of the Triumph of Bacchus found on these coolers was probably made into working designs for the Storr workshop by John Flaxman RA. One of these drawings is in the collection of the Victoria and Albert Museum, contained in a folio labelled "Designs for Plate by John Flaxman etc." Another candidate for authorship, however, is the head of Rundell's design team, William Theed.

The Medici Vase was one of the great inspirations of Renaissance and later art. A monumental bell-shaped *krater*, it is believed to have been sculpted in Athens in the second half of the first century AD. Some five feet high, its sides are carved with a mythological bas-relief which has defied precise identification over the centuries. A half-draped female figure, apparently Iphigenia, is seated below a statue of a goddess, possibly Diana, while heroic warriors look on. They are perhaps Agamemnon and either Achilles or Odysseus.

The vase appears in a 1598 inventory of the Villa Medici in Rome, but its earlier history is unknown. It was moved to Florence in 1780 and since then it has been displayed in the Uffizi Gallery. During the past four hundred years it has been the subject of innumerable paintings as well as engravings, the most famous of which is one by Stefano della Bella of 1656. It often featured in *capricci* or composed views that were a specialty of the Roman painter Giovanni Paolo Panini and others. Angelica Kaufmann painted the 2nd Lord Berwick on his Grand Tour seated beside the vase.

Four **wine coasters**

Silver gilt, wood
London, 1822
Maker's mark of **Joseph Cradock & William Reid**
Diameter: 7½ in (19 cm)

HERALDY
The crest is that of Teixeira for Henrique Teixeira de Sampaio, Baron of Teixeira, later 1st Count of Póvoa (1774–1833).

PROVENANCE
Henrique Teixeira de Sampaio, Baron of Teixeira and later 1st Count of Póvoa (1774–1833), then by descent to his son João Maria de Noronha, 2nd Count of Póvoa (1826–1837), on whose death the titles became extinct and the family fortunes and his silver passed to his sister Marie Louise de Noronha Sampaio, who married Domingos António Pedro de Sousa Holstein, later the 2nd Duke of Palmela (1818–1864)
By descent in the family of the dukes of Palmela at Casa Palmela in Portugal

EXHIBITED
Lisbon, 2001: *Una Familía de Coleccionadores: Poder e Cultura*, Casa-Museu Doutor Anastácio Gonçalves, February–September 2001, two coasters exhibited

PUBLISHED
Maria Antónia Pinto de Matos and Maria de Sousa e Holstein Campilho, eds., *Una Familía de Coleccionadores: Poder e Cultura*, exh. cat., Lisbon, 2001, p. 224

In the 1820s, the Baron of Teixeira was the richest man in Portugal. The foundation of his wealth had been the lucrative contracts he had had to supply the Anglo-Portuguese forces with food during the Peninsula War. He went on to provide loans to the Portuguese government, so that by 1820 he was the state's largest creditor. In 1823 he was created Count of Póvoa and it may be have been to mark this occasion that he purchased an extensive dinner service, in white silver as well as silver gilt, from the leading goldsmiths of London including Paul Storr.

16

Coffee pot

Silver gilt, ebony, ivory
Paris, 1798–1809
Maker's mark of **Martin-Guillaume Biennais**
Height: 8⅛ in (20.6 cm)
Gross weight: 15 oz (466 g)

PROVENANCE
Sotheby's, London, 12 March 1962, lot 53
C. Ruxton Love, New York City
The Audrey B. Love Foundation, Christie's, New York,
14 June 1982, lot 135
Christie's, Geneva, 13 November 1990, lot 83

PUBLISHED
The Ivory Hammer: The Year at Sotheby's 219th Season 1962–1963, London, 1963, p. 175
Vanessa Brett, *The Sotheby's Directory of Silver, 1600–1940*, London, 1986, pp. 370–1, no. 1767

Friezes of swans and peacocks became a popular feature of Empire decoration from 1800 onwards. They feature in the published designs of Percier and Fontaine, notably their *Recueil de décorations intérieures*. The swans are perhaps inspired by those which support a tripod brazier in Jacques-Louis David's picture *Les Amours de Pâris et d'Hélène* painted as early as 1788. Seized from the comte d'Artois during the Revolution, the painting is now in the Louvre.

Pair of verrières

Silver gilt
Paris, 1809–1819
Maker's mark of Jean-Baptiste-Claude Odiot
Width: 15 in (38 cm)
Weight: 103 oz (3,196 g)

The *verrière* made its appearance as the successor to the monteith during the late eighteenth century. Typically elliptical and with either drop ring or loop handles, it was intended to be filled with ice or cold water to allow inverted glasses to be suspended from the notched rim. They were a prominent feature in most of the grand silver-gilt services produced by Odiot in the early nineteenth century.

18

Equestrian **punch bowl**

Silver gilt
London, 1831
Maker's mark of **Paul Storr**
Height: 10¼ in (26 cm)
Weight: 109 oz (3,390 g)

The so-called Warwick Vase provided the inspiration for this bowl. Dug up in the grounds of Hadrian's Villa in the eighteenth century, the magnificent Roman *krater* was as renowned as the Medici Vase, now in the Uffizi in Florence (see cat. no. 14).

19

The **Glastonbury Cup**: an historicist **tankard**

Silver gilt
London 1820
Maker's mark of **Philip Rundell**
Height: 8½ in (21.5 cm)
Weight: 101 oz (3,141 g)

HERALDRY
The arms are those of Arundell of Wardour, for James Everard, 10th Baron Arundell of Wardour (1785–1834).

PROVENANCE
James Everard, 10th Baron Arundell of Wardour (1785–1834)
By descent to R.J.R. Arundell, Esq., Christie's, London, 12 March 1969, lot 30
Bulgari, Rome

PUBLISHED
Shirley Bury, *et al*. "The Antiquarian Plate of George IV: a Gloss on E.A. Jones", *The Burlington Magazine*, June, 1979, p. 348 and footnote

This extraordinary tankard is a cast of the so-called "Glastonbury Cup" from the collection of Lord Arundell of Wardour Castle. The exact history of when the cup entered the Arundell family is unclear. Tradition has it that it was taken from Glastonbury Abbey in Somerset at the time of the dissolution of the monasteries by Henry VIII. However, the earliest record of its being with the family is during the English Civil war.

The "Glastonbury Cup" became famous in the eighteenth century, when it was published in "Observations on an Ancient Cup" in *Archaelogia* in 1794 and it continued to grow in renown into the nineteenth. Indeed by 1825 it was so well known that Thomas Dudley Fosbroke used it as the example to define the peg-tankard, describing them thus:

> The peg-tankards … had in the inside a row of eight pins one above another from top to bottom; the tankards hold two quarts, so that there is a gill of ale, i.e. half a pint Winchester measure, between each pin. The first person that drank was to empty the tankard to the first peg, or pin; the second to the next pin, &c. by which means the pins were so many measures to the compotators, making them all drink alike, or the same quantity …

The Glastonbury Cup.
Image courtesy of Glastonbury Abbey

20

Pair of four-light **candelabra**

Silver gilt
London, 1832
Maker's mark of **Paul Storr**,
retailed by Storr & Mortimer
Stamped STORR & MORTIMER on the base
Height: 18 in (46 cm)
Gross weight: 239 oz (7,160 g)

PROVENANCE
Roger Makins, 1st Baron Sherfield (1904–1996), British
Ambassador to Washington, 1953–1956

These most unusual candelabra can be seen as the last phase of the Egyptomania of the early nineteenth century (see cat. no. 5). Their clustered stems have alternating convex and concave sections. Their construction is also distinctive. The decoration of anthemion and scrolls on the bases is cast in sections and each component has been hallmarked as have the rims of the bases.

21

Pair of Flaxman **ewers**

Silver gilt
London, 1904
Maker's mark of **Elkington & Co.**
Height: 16½ in (42 cm)
Weight: 245 oz (7,620 g)

PROVENANCE
Maharanee of Baroda, until 1983
Private collection, France

The design for these ewers is based on a pair of plaster vases, one decorated with a triton and one with a satyr, symbolizing water and wine, exhibited at the Académie de Saint-Luc in Paris in 1774 by Sigisbert-François Michel (1728–1811), nephew of the sculptor Claude Michel, known as Clodion (1738–1814). The English sculptor John Flaxman adapted the design for Josiah Wedgwood, whose factory produced versions in his famous black basalt from the 1770s onwards. Silver versions, however, are scarce.

22

Pair of four-light **candelabra**

Silver gilt
London, 1850
Maker's mark of **Robert Garrard & Co.**
Height: 26 in (66 cm)
Weight: 438 oz (13,620 g)

These candelabra are in the *Régence* taste, based on early eighteenth-century candlesticks by Huguenot makers. As early as the 1820s the form was being revived by the Royal Goldsmiths, Rundell, Bridge & Rundell, and their chief rivals, Garrard's.

In 1809, Robert Garrard II was apprenticed to his father, Robert Garrard I, a partner of Wakelin & Company, and gained his freedom of the Grocers' Company by patrimony in 1816. After the death of his father in 1818, Garrard entered his mark and, with his brothers James and Sebastian, took over the management of the workshop. During the early nineteenth century, the firm's business expanded at a tremendous rate, especially after the decline of Rundell, Bridge & Rundell in the 1820s. In 1830, Garrard's were appointed goldsmiths and jewellers to the king and in 1843 official crown jewellers. A large design studio was set up by them, which was modelled on that developed by Rundell, Bridge & Rundell and employed several well-known painters and sculptors, including Edmund Cotterill. During the mid-nineteenth century, Garrard's was one of the leading producers of elaborate presentation silver.

Photographed by Guy Hills at Raynham Hall, Norfolk, by kind permission of the Marquess and Marchioness Townshend, and at another Norfolk location. Appearances by Bob and Blackjack

Special thanks to Mick Ace

Designed by Chris Jones, Design4Science Ltd

Printed in Italy by Conti Tipocolor, Florence

Published for Koopman Rare Art by John Adamson,
90 Hertford Street, Cambridge CB4 3AQ, England

ISBN: 978-1-898565-12-3

© 2013 Koopman Rare Art